TITANIC

In a New Light

Propellers and rudder of the Titanic's *identical sister ship* Olympic.

Titanic's *starboard wing propeller.*

RMS Titanic.

TITANIC

In a New Light

Dr. Joseph MacInnis

THOMASSON-GRANT
Charlottesville, Virginia

First-class smoking room.

Published by Thomasson-Grant, Inc.
Designed by Leonard G. Phillips
Edited by Susie Shulman
Copyright © 1992 Dr. Joseph B. MacInnis
All rights reserved.
This book, or any portions thereof, may not be reproduced in any form
without written permission from the publisher.
Color separations by Koford International Pte. Ltd., Singapore.
Printed and bound in the United States by R. R. Donnelley & Sons.

99 98 97 96 95 94 93 92   5 4 3 2 1

Any inquiries should be directed to Thomasson-Grant, Inc.
One Morton Drive, Suite 500, Charlottesville, VA 22903-6806
(804) 977-1780

Library of Congress
Cataloging-in-Publication Data

MacInnis, Joseph B.
    Titanic in a new light / Joseph MacInnis
        p.   cm.
    ISBN 1-56566-025-0   — ISBN 1-56566-021-8 (pbk.)
    1. Titanic (Steamship) 2. Shipwrecks—North Atlantic Ocean.
    3. Underwater exploration—North Atlantic Ocean. I. Title.
    G530.T6M23 1992
    910' .91631—dc20   92-22682
                                                    CIP

CONTENTS

The submersible Mir 1 *touches down on the boat deck opposite* Mir 2. *The forward wall frame of the Titanic's wheelhouse runs under the subs. To the right is the telemotor steering control. The lights, boomed out on both sides of each sub, are the brightest ever used in the deep sea.*

TWO-AND-A-HALF MILES BENEATH THE NORTH ATLANTIC, I AM PARKED ON THE BRIDGE DECK OF THE *TITANIC* IN A SMALL RUSSIAN SUBMARINE.

Through the viewport I can see the gleaming bronze shaft of the telemotor steering control, the device that directed the *Titanic* toward her fatal rendezvous with the iceberg. On the other side of the telemotor is a twin submarine, its brilliant lights slicing through the blackness like flares shot from the sun.

The lights represent a new dawn in deep-ocean exploration. Designed specifically for this expedition, they have allowed us to see, as if for the first time, the world's most famous shipwreck. Since it was discovered in 1985, the *Titanic* has been visible only as a still photograph or a video image confined to the small screen. But inside the twin submarine is an IMAX motion-picture camera, which, in combination with the special lights, will project the huge ship almost life-size on a screen more than 3,000 times as big as a television screen.

This book is about the expedition that "captured" the *Titanic* and brought her to life in the IMAX format. Its chapters highlight historic and personal elements of the story. But this is primarily a picture book, presenting the world's most advanced deep-ocean filming system and the men who operate it, and sharing the results of their efforts—fascinating new pictures of the Mount Everest of shipwrecks.

It is a story complete with characters and motivations that is even more dramatically expressed in Stephen Low's IMAX film, *Titanica*.

I watch intently as the other sub, its lights diminishing like an echo, lifts off and heads toward the half-square-mile debris field between the bow and the stern. On this, the last dive of the expedition, we have placed three plaques beside the telemotor, in memory of those who perished and in recognition of those who survived the sinking of the great ship *Titanic* on that clear, dark night in the icy North Atlantic.

This book is for them,
and for all those
who made this expedition possible.

Filmmaker Stephen Low describes the set-up of an IMAX shot to expedition leader Anatoly Sagalevitch aboard the 6,000-ton Akademik Keldysh, *home to the 130 members of the expedition and mother ship to the two Mir submersibles.*

A Convergence of Currents

I MADE MY FIRST TRIP TO THE SOVIET UNION IN THE FALL OF 1973, TRAVELING ON A NEW SCIENTIFIC EXCHANGE PROGRAM BETWEEN CANADA AND THE USSR.

In Moscow and Leningrad, I showed a short film to my fellow scientists about my diving research work under the polar ice cap. The film, by Canada's National Film Board, told the story of how we built a small transparent work station under the ice in freezing water. The Russians loved it. For the first time I discovered how the synergy of science and film could bring people closer together.

Two years earlier, an extraordinary new film theater opened in Toronto, not far from where I live. Inside a white geodesic dome built over the water of Lake Ontario were 800 seats in front of a screen seven stories high. As I looked at the color and clarity of the huge IMAX images in a film about Lake Superior, I realized I was looking at the ultimate way of sharing the experience of exploring the ocean.

Late in the summer of 1980, a team I was leading found the world's northernmost known shipwreck under the ice of the Northwest Passage. That same summer, Jack Grimm, a Texas oilman, began his three-year search for the *Titanic*. He did not find it, but he surveyed the seafloor, laying the groundwork for future expeditions. Five years later, the ruins of the *Titanic* were found. In 1987, in the French submarine *Nautile*, I had my first closeup look at the world's most famous shipwreck. As I looked out the sub's small viewport, I realized that the only way to "raise" this ship was to capture it on 70-mm, 15-perforation film and place it, life-size, on the dozens of IMAX screens around the world.

Several other people shared this dream: *National Geographic* photographer Emory Kristof, filmmaker Stephen Low, André Picard of Imax Corporation, and, in the Soviet Union, Dr. Anatoly Sagalevitch.

In 1987, the prestigious Shirshov Institute in Moscow launched a pair of small research submarines. Built at a cost of $50 million, they were the most advanced in the world. Later that year, Dr. Sagalevitch wrote an article in a technical journal asking Western scientists to join him and his group in the exploration of the deep sea. At Emory Kristof's house in Washington, D.C., we agreed to take the first tentative step.

During the next two years, Sagalevitch, Kristof, and I worked together on a number of projects. On a transatlantic voyage aboard a Russian research ship, we dove the two subs into a canyon to a depth of 16,400 feet. In Siberia, we explored the steep floor of Lake Baikal, the world's oldest and deepest lake.

It was a fragile alliance. The Berlin Wall, that concrete symbol of the Cold War, was still standing. We did not really comprehend one another's language or ideology. But, on the slanting, wind-swept deck of the research vessel that harbored the subs, sharing the challenge of exploring the sea, we were compelled to know one another. And in the cramped quarters of a small sub three miles under the ocean, there were no alternatives except trust and teamwork.

In June of 1990, I brought Sagalevitch and his colleague, Professor Y. Yastrebov, to Toronto. We sat down with Stephen Low and André Picard in the same theater where I had seen my first IMAX film 18 years earlier. This was an important moment for Stephen: for years he had been obsessed with the idea of placing the world's biggest shipwreck on the world's biggest screen.

After looking at the stunning images of a new film called *To The Limit*, we committed ourselves to an expedition and film. We knew we had a story that would change forever humankind's view of the deep ocean. We also hoped that working together would make a small contribution toward world peace.

For the next year we fought our way through a bewildering agenda. At times, the financial and technical problems seemed as immutable as the ocean that surrounded the ship. How would we finance the project? Would the Russians be ready, given the unsettled conditions within their country? How were we going to illuminate a giant ship resting in two-and-a-half miles of darkness?

These and hundreds of other problems inspired an Olympic-team effort. A small group headed by André Picard somehow solved the financial challenge. As his country melted away into separate republics, Dr. Anatoly Sagalevitch managed to refurbish his research ship and two submersibles in time to sail to the Bermuda rendezvous point. In Washington and Woods Hole, Emory Kristof and Chris Nicholson put together a team that broke all records building a unique set of deep-sea lights.

In the final months of preparation, two more major elements were added. Steve Blasco, a geologist from the Geological Survey of Canada, became the expedition's chief scientist. And, prompted by producer/director Al Giddings, the CBS network committed to producing a one-hour television special.

The sinking of the *Titanic* in 1912 has inspired dozens of cinematic interpretations of the ship's tragic end. As the pieces of the complex expedition came slowly and painstakingly together, it became clear to Stephen Low that the expedition itself was an intriguing subject for a film. Its cast of scientists and technical experts, their fascination with the giant shipwreck, all set against the backdrop of a Russian research ship and the drama of the deep sea, was the stuff of science fiction; to Low, the challenge of bringing the whole experience to the IMAX screen was irresistible.

The film would weave together several stories: the creation of the *Titanic* in the shipyard of Harland and Wolff, the story of the ship's sinking as recounted by survivor Eva Hart, and the adventure of an international expedition to the ship's deep-sea resting place.

Almost a year to the day after the commitment in Toronto, an excited group of adventurers stood assembled on the deck of a Russian ship in Bermuda.

Some 600 miles to the north, another ship, split in two and sleeping on the sediments for nearly 80 years, lay waiting.

One of the many planning sessions held on board the Keldysh *en route to the dive site. From left to right: Al Giddings, Ralph White, Anatoly Sagalevitch, Emory Kristof, Genya Chernyaev, Nikolai Shushkov, and Andrei Andreev.*

The bow of the Keldysh cuts through the North Atlantic on her way to the dive site.

CHAPTER ONE

The North Atlantic

THE YEAR WAS 1912. ON A BRISK
APRIL AFTERNOON,
THE *TITANIC* STEAMED
ALONG THE SOUTHERN
COAST OF IRELAND,
HER BROAD DECKS
OPEN TO THE BREEZE.

Off her starboard side were the shadowy cliffs of the Old Head of Kinsale. Ahead lay 3,000 miles of empty ocean.

The North Atlantic is a space so vast it cannot be defined by oceanography. An eternal source of fascination and fear, it is regarded by mariners as the grayest, meanest stretch of water on the planet.

On the topographic maps that show the oceanic crust laid bare, the North Atlantic is dominated by the peaks of a central mountain range that runs southward from Iceland. Discovered more than 100 years ago, this immense line of peaks, at least a mile under the surface and more than twice as long as the Rockies, divides the North Atlantic into two roughly parallel troughs.

The crest of this mountain range holds an ancient valley—a geographical ax cut—15 to 30 miles wide. Deep in the bottom of the valley, where the heat of the mantle is pressing upward, the earth is turning itself inside out. Partially molten material is rising in irregular pulses, spreading apart and moving toward Europe and America at the rate of about one inch per year. This process, which is creating oceanic crust, has been going on for 200 million years and accounts for the present width of the North Atlantic. It also accounts for the fact that the thousands of ships that are on the bottom, the fires in their boilers long extinguished, are still sluggishly proceeding toward a distant shore.

In addition to the central mountain range, there are two dominant levels in the relief of the North Atlantic. As the *Titanic* sailed west, leaving the coast of Ireland behind, she passed over the submerged continental shelf, which begins at the shoreline and runs seaward to a depth of 600 feet. The abyssal plains, the second level, lie at an average depth of 12,000 feet. Altogether, the shelves and the plains and the steep slopes that connect them are enveloped by more than ten million square miles of seawater.

It is the seamless struggle between oceanic currents and atmospheric weather systems that gives the North Atlantic its intimidating reputation. Within hours it can switch from a plain of pearly mists to a place where waves are as high as a house. The destructive forces of wind and wave expose the slightest flaw in a ship's structure or the vigilance of her crew. Winter storms are the worst. Even today, the quarterly issues of the mariner's weather log enumerate the casualties. The container ship *Tuxpan* disappeared with 27 on board. The *Balsa* capsized with its crew of 19. The semisubmersible drilling rig *Ocean Ranger* sank in a storm on the Grand Banks, capsized by 50-foot waves and winds of 109 mph; all 84 hands were lost. The next day, only a few miles away, the same storm claimed a Soviet container ship.

In the early spring of 1912, the *Titanic* sailed west for four days across an untroubled sea. The sky was clear, and the sea through which she traced her long, white wake was calm. By Sunday noon, April 14, she had covered almost 1,500 miles.

Under her humming keel was the turbulent ocean, driven by a host of forces. The deepest water, the thousands of square miles blanketing the abyssal plains, had its origins in the Arctic east of Greenland. Here, the polar waters increase their density by cooling and taking on salt from ice. In the process, they begin a long, voluminous slide toward the south, where they guard the ocean floor in temperatures close to freezing.

The surface currents of the North Atlantic are primarily wind driven. Between 10° and 30° latitude, easterly winds drive the great waters toward America. Farther from the equator, between 40° and 60° latitude, where the *Titanic* was sailing, westerly winds push them toward Europe. This huge, roughly circular pattern, with its thousands of swirling rings, eddies, and meanders, is called the North Atlantic Gyre.

In the southwestern section of the Gyre, where horizons of whitecaps press against the flank of Florida, the surface waters have merged into a narrow, northbound current called the Gulf Stream. Off Cape Hatteras, where its width is 40 miles, the Gulf Stream extends to depths of nearly 3,300 feet. Farther north it meets the westerly winds that push it offshore. South of Newfoundland's Grand Banks, where the *Titanic*

was heading en route to New York, the Gulf Stream disperses and becomes less stable.

It is in this area that the North Atlantic is famed for its sudden free falls in visibility. Here, where the Gulf Stream embraces the Labrador Current, warm air collides with a cold sea, suspending billions of minute water droplets at eye level. In really thick fog, when texture gradients and other visual clues are lost, sea captains slow their ships and turn in haste to their electronic instruments.

Mimicking the stealth of the Vikings, other invaders slide in from the north. They are the icebergs—blocky, tabulated, crenelated—as many as 15,000 a year. Calved where Greenland's glaciers meet the sea, they are borne south on the Labrador Current wearing colors that range from white to green to blue. A few of them, laced by soil or rocks, are brown or black. Even with 90 percent of their mass hidden under the sea, some icebergs are as high as Westminster Abbey. Others are low, and as long as a city block. As the poor souls on the *Titanic* were to find out, at night, hidden in the shadows of a moonless sea, icebergs can be ship killers.

North Atlantic iceberg.

THE NIGHT WE CANNOT FORGET

It happened at 11:40 P.M. as the *Titanic* steamed through the cold, calm sea at 20.5 knots. The incalculable iceberg, towering some 60 feet above the water, lay dead ahead.

The iceberg broke through the hull plates along the starboard bow; within minutes the great ship was drifting helplessly, taking on huge amounts of water.

At 12:45 A.M., the first lifeboat, Number Seven, was lowered half full. Many others were lowered without being filled to capacity.

At 1:30 A.M., a wireless message was sent into the darkness: "We are sinking fast . . . cannot last much longer."

By 2:20 A.M., the ship had broken in two, and survivors watched as the stern slowly followed the bow downward and disappeared. More than 1,500 people were lost in what has been termed the greatest maritime tragedy in history.

The apparent emptiness of the North Atlantic masks the complexities of its appalling depths. The pieces of the broken ship fell through the upper layers and continued downward. Then they dropped through a realm of permanent darkness inhabited by grotesque and improbable creatures. The *Titanic* came to rest in about two-and-a-half miles of water, a distance that coincides with the average depth of the world's oceans. It is a zone marked by extremes of cold, pressure, and darkness.

The main bridge telegraph, used to send signals from the bridge to the engine room, lies in the debris field, one-quarter-mile behind the bridge. Its position reader indicator reads "slow ahead."

FACING *A section of the fallen foremast just above the crow's nest, where lookout Fred Fleet was standing when he picked up the phone and reported to the bridge, "Iceberg right ahead!" A broken cable that once helped support the mast now hangs straight down. The hole with the black wires running through it is the small hatch through which the lookouts climbed to enter and exit the crow's nest.*

Titanic *in her slip during the final preparations for launching. An indica-
tion of her gigantic size is given by the man leaning against the railing.*

CHAPTER TWO

Building a Legend

THE *TITANIC* WAS BORN
IN BELFAST,
AT THE EDGE OF
THE IRISH SEA,
UNDER A STEEL-WEBBED
GANTRY AS HIGH
AS A CATHEDRAL.

The top of the gantry, built to lift enormous channel beams and castings into place, offered a panoramic view of the smokestacks of Belfast, the river Lagan, and 2,000 acres of graving decks, dry docks, plating sheds, foundries, timber yards, boiler shops, stables, mold lofts, mast sheds, engine works, erecting and fitting sheds, an electricity-generating station, and a red-bricked, three-story main office building. Awash in soot and steam and filled with thousands of smudge-faced men, this noisy riverside kingdom was the celebrated Queen's Island yard of Harland and Wolff, shipbuilders to the world.

Late in the morning of March 31, 1909, under a gray sky and the latticed girders of this 6,000-ton gantry, a gang of Irishmen wearing tweed caps finished pounding home the final section of a ribbon of steel as wide as a man's chest and 850 feet long. Slanting down a gentle incline toward the black waters of the river Lagan was the backbone of a new ship—RMS *Titanic*.

In the days that followed, the "Islandmen" of Harland and Wolff riveted a five-foot-high vertical keel plate on top of the strip

Flag of the White Star Line, owners of the Titanic.

of continuous metal. As spring became summer, a flat double bottom grew out of both sides of the keel, 90 feet across at its widest point and tapering toward the bow and stern. To brace the floor of the *Titanic*, huge plates of steel were riveted in double, triple, and in some places, quadruple seams.

Like all the ships built at the turn of the century, the *Titanic* was held together by a six-ounce piece of metal that could be cradled in the palm of a man's hand. Fired to red heat, the "button-head" rivet was driven through two holes in overlapping metal plates. The part of the shaft that extended beyond the plates was hydraulically compressed into a second hemispherical head. As the rivet cooled, it shrank and pulled the two plates together. The *Titanic*, like her sister ship *Olympic*, was built for extended combat with the sea. Altogether, three million rivets, weighing 1,200 tons, were used to lock the ship into one gigantic piece. A third of these, one million rivets, weighing 270 tons, were used to fortify the double bottom.

On April 6, 1910, a year after her keel was laid, the 10,000

The construction gantry in the north yard at Harland and Wolff was 840 feet long, 270 feet wide, and 230 feet high. The Titanic *was born in the left slip, the* Olympic *in the right.*

Some of the "Islandmen" of the Harland and Wolff shipyards in Belfast, Ireland, where the Titanic *and her sister ship* Olympic *(featured in most of the following construction photographs) were built. Posing for their portrait under the port wing propeller, these were but a few of the approximately 10,000 men, representing dozens of skills and trades, who helped build the ships over a three-year period.*

TOP *Steam boilers lined up in the Harland and Wolff boiler shop. The Titanic had 24 double-ended and five single-ended boilers. Each of the double-ended boilers was 20 feet long and contained six coal-burning furnaces.*

ABOVE *The web frame construction down near the turn of the bilge. The outer skin is partially plated; the inner skin is not yet plated.*

Turbine rotor being moved in the shop.

riveters, joiners, carpenters, shipwrights, and yardmen building the *Titanic* looked up through the haze of the shipyard and saw the steel skeleton of their ship. Rising from both sides of the double bottom like the ribs of a mastodon were 350 frames that would give the new vessel its penetrating shape.

The rise from the keel to the boat deck matched the height of a ten-story building. A distance of two city blocks lay between the bow and the stern. And inside the frames was enough space to contain most of the concrete poured into Hoover Dam.

The interior of this leviathan now resembled the steel bones of an 85-story hotel lying on its side. From the double bottom upward, the Islandmen had hoisted into the sky ten levels of deck beams, stringers, strong beams, support columns, channel beams, bracket knees, and steel plates, some weighing more than a ton, each fixed into place by swarms of sweating men working under the shadows of a dozen cranes shuttling the length and width of the gantry high above them.

One by one, the steel plates that formed the outer hull were bullied into position. Each was about six feet high, 30 feet long, and weighed up to 6,000 pounds. In mid-October of that year, 5,060 plates, enough to cover the field and parking lot at Yankee Stadium, were hoisted and hot-riveted into place. The shell of the *Titanic*, its first defense against the ambiguities of the sea, was complete.

Turbine casing in the engine works.

SHE IS LAUNCHED

For the next seven months, the Islandmen raced to finish the major steelwork of the interior—the floors, walls, and ceilings that, after she was launched, would become staterooms, dining rooms, boiler rooms, and engine rooms. Then, on May 31, 1911, in front of 100,000 spectators, the *Titanic*, painted black and weighing 25,000 tons, was released to the sea.

This first journey, on a bubbling smear of 23 tons of tallow, train oil, and soap, took 62 seconds. As she slid wheezing and screeching down the wooden incline, the *Titanic* achieved a maximum velocity of twelve-and-a-half knots. The shoreline fluttered with the flags, bunting, and banners of well-wishers; on both sides of the river, strong voices shouted for her safety and success.

After her launch, the *Titanic* was moored to the Belfast harbor's deepwater wharf. A 200-ton crane, one of the world's biggest, was nudged alongside. For the next ten months, the arm of this crane fed into the new ship a steady stream of boilers, refrigerators, reciprocating engines, filters, and condensers. So substantial was this avalanche of iron and steel that, from launch to sea trials, the *Titanic* doubled her weight.

During the summer that followed, 29 high-pressure boilers, each the size of a one-story building, were lowered through framed holes in the decks. One by one, they were bolted to the double

Crankshafts for the two main reciprocating engines on the floor of the engine shop.

bottom in five rows of five abreast. In boiler room number six, where the hull began to taper toward the bow, there was room for only four.

HER ENGINES

The two biggest spaces in the ship were a pair of cavernous rooms between the boilers and propellers. Into the forward room a pair of reciprocating engines, each with the girth and smell of a locomotive, was lowered and bolted down side by side. The bedplate beneath each one weighed 195 tons. Their low-pressure cylinders were eight feet across. The second room, closer to the propellers, was filled with a 430-ton Parson steam turbine.

The 50,000-ton *Titanic* was designed to be driven by steam blasting out of the boilers at 215 pounds per square inch of pressure. Racing through a series of wide-bore pipes, the steam would cascade from the high- to the intermediate- and into the low-pressure cylinders of the two reciprocating engines. Then it would roar across the spinning blades of the turbine. Crankshafts and propellers would turn. The steam would be condensed and returned to the boilers. Harland and Wolff engineers calculated that when the steam system was running at full throttle, the engines would produce a driving power of 46,000 horses.

TOP *First-class grand staircase leading down to A deck.*

LEFT *First-class Café Parisienne on B deck.*

READY FOR THE SEA

Completion of the lavish Edwardian interior of the *Titanic* required hundreds of carpenters, electricians, plumbers, and painters working for months simultaneously on all ten decks. In late March, when the last worker walked down the gangplank, he left behind a sublime extravaganza of skylights, reception rooms, grand staircases, stained-glass windows, dining rooms, chandeliers, smoking rooms, libraries, restaurants, reading rooms, a Turkish bath, a gymnasium and swimming pool, and 762 first-, second-, and third-class staterooms—the whole labyrinthine assembly connected by more than five miles of passageways, elevators, stairwells, and corridors.

On April 2, 1912, her brief sea trials completed, the *Titanic* steamed out of Belfast harbor, turned south, and headed toward Southampton. Like every ship built during the past 10,000 years of seafaring, she was an empirical experiment in how to confront the eccentricities of the sea. For onlookers and officers alike, there was something about her massiveness that hinted of invincibility. She was the largest moving object ever built by human hands, and she floated on a floor of double-riveted steel. But like so many large and complex experiments, the *Titanic* had a flaw. She had been conceived by a small group of ambitious men who intended to confront Poseidon without knowing exactly who he was.

The **Titanic** *pulls away from the White Star dock in Southampton, England, at the start of her maiden voyage on April 10, 1912. The upper decks were filled with first-class passengers from some of the wealthiest English and American families of the day. Far below, in the heat and grime of the boiler rooms, an army of stokers and trimmers muscled coal from the bunkers into the furnaces.*

Eva Hart, age 7, with her parents Benjamin and Esther. The photograph was taken at their home in England a few weeks before the family sailed on the Titanic.

FACING *Eva, age 86, in a photograph taken a few months after the expedition, at her home in England. She is holding a French bulldog similar to one she befriended on the ship.*

CHAPTER THREE

Eva's Story

"IF THERE HAD ONLY BEEN ENOUGH LIFEBOATS... A CALM SEA, A STARLIT NIGHT, AND TWO-AND-A-HALF HOURS FROM THE TIME OF IMPACT TO THE TIME SHE SANK... PLENTY OF TIME TO SAVE EVERYONE, IF ONLY WE HAD ENOUGH LIFEBOATS...."

She was seven years old when it happened. Shivering in Number 14 lifeboat, looking across a charcoal sea at the stern of the *Titanic* against a puzzling array of stars, she felt the percussive shudder. She heard the competing thunders coming from somewhere beneath the surface. She watched as the great ship, its radiance exhausted, slid out of sight with the weight of a dislodged mountain. It has been 80 years since these things happened, but Eva Hart clearly remembers opening her lips in a silent scream of terror.

The air temperature was freezing and the water temperature not much above that, and from somewhere in the outer darkness, out of the lungs of the hundreds of men and women and children still alive in the freezing ocean, came a chorus of moans and howls, a collective explosion of breath that was palpable to all who heard it. Eva did not know it—the realization would come later when she was older—but one of the screams, falling like a feather from the sky, came from her drowning father.

She last saw him in his dark overcoat, standing at the railing looking down into her lifeboat.

"He leaned over and said, 'Be a good girl and hold onto Mommy's hand—'" she recalls.

Eva's mother, Esther, her face white as a candle, was sitting beside her in the lifeboat, every molecule yearning for some sign of her husband, Benjamin.

Eva continues, "He used to say he could swim before he could walk. I can remember him saying, 'There's one thing about it, they can't drown me; I'll never drown.'"

Eva still winces inwardly when she tells her story. Like all who hold painful childhood memories, she defends herself with a mixture of selective amnesia and wishful thinking. Over the past eight decades, her story has evolved into a vivid, articulate, organized dream.

That long April night in 1912 has spawned hundreds of books, songs, and films and countless essays and opinions. No other story about the sea has been told and retold so many times. The authors are part of a larger audience, this century's witnesses to one of the great human tragedies. Somehow, they have sensed that in trying to comprehend the events—the plot and the characters and how they met their fate—they can learn more about humankind, more about themselves. To confront the *Titanic* is to confront one's own mortality.

THE END OF INNOCENCE

For Eva Hart, those blinding, burning hours on a cold, black sea meant the end of innocence.

"I had an enormous teddy bear my father had bought for me the Christmas before we went away. It was almost as tall as I was. I loved it and I used to play with it on the deck with my father, and the captain stopped several times and commented on my teddy bear and spoke to my father, who was delighted with him. He was an awfully nice man.

"I wanted to go back for my teddy bear when my father was carrying me out of the cabin to take me up to the boat deck. I remember saying, 'I want my teddy bear!' He didn't say anything; he just continued to carry me.

"I never had another teddy bear. I never wanted another one."

A SURREAL DREAM

When the *Titanic* perished in front of Eva Hart, its imaginary life persisted, a kind of exoskeleton that continued to float long after the glass and steel had gone. One of the elements that most impresses her is how clearly her mother anticipated the events that would unfold.

"She had a terrible premonition about safety. She didn't know what, just this awful premonition of danger. She felt she should not go to sleep at night, but stayed awake, sitting in her chair, knitting.

"It was only because she was wide awake and wakened my father, who was very cross about going

A woman's shoe in the debris field.

up on deck because she had done it before. But she made him go up, and she wakened me. He came straight back for us, and so my mother and I were in plenty of time to get into a lifeboat."

For Eva and the rest of the survivors, the experience was surreal, a series of bizarre images, puzzling juxtapositions, and gaps in time and continuity.

The itinerant alp of an iceberg, drifting down from Greenland, hiding in its own shadows . . .

The British officers—a row of pale faces in the wheelhouse, eyes bulging, breath rapid—trying not to reveal surprise or dismay . . .

Fifteen watertight doors slamming shut. The brainless flow of tons of water—cold, clear green, the color of glacier water—into the ship through a hole in the bow . . .

The front of the great ship, its lights blazing, being drawn toward the center of the earth . . .

The realization that all the plans and drawings, all the engineering and craftsmanship, all the maritime experience and seamanship—simply did not work . . .

As Eva's lifeboat drifted south in the starry darkness, the *Titanic* was being pulled down into her

The stem of the bow deeply embedded in the seafloor. The starboard anchor is in the shadows on the left, with the sediments forced upward to within seven feet of the flukes. To see how deeply the bow of the Titanic *is buried, notice the distance between the anchor and the keel in the photograph on page 22.*

grave. After separating from the stern, the front half of the ship slid forward, still upright, under one and then two miles of water. At two-and-a-half miles, the bow and double bottom found the seafloor, driving full-tilt, head-on, into the sediments. The stern section, freighted with tons of engines and machinery, plunged almost straight down into the homicidal depths. Half a mile of brown sediment lay between them. Since the two ends of the great ship were no longer joined by any physical bond, fragments and sections, contents of the interior, ripped, broke, spilled, fluttered, and sank in all directions. The heaviest pieces sank first. By 8:30 A.M., when Eva and the last boatload of survivors had been taken aboard the rescue ship *Carpathia*, most of the lighter objects, including clothing, had relaxed into the abyss.

Eva Hart feels strongly that we must not forget the *Titanic* and what the tragedy taught us: "A long time has gone by since she sank and many things have happened in the world, but I do feel that the 1,500 people that died that night . . . must remain in our memories as a perfect example of man's arrogance. And this will go on . . . people will think they have invented something perfect . . . like a ship that wouldn't sink. We've got to be reminded that that's not so—and I think the *Titanic* will always be the biggest reminder of all."

Swimming in the slow motion so characteristic of this nearly frozen world, a rat-tail fish leads Mir 2 along the hull plates of the bow toward the 7³/4-ton starboard anchor. The rat-tail was one of 28 species of animals found living on or near the wreck.

The port and starboard anchor windlass drums stand silently on the forecastle deck in front of the number one hatch. A section of anchor chain can be seen leading forward from the starboard windlass.

FACING *One of the capstan drums on the forecastle deck. Topped with bronze, the drum was used to haul in heavy lines as the vessel was warped alongside the dock.*

CHAPTER FOUR

The Silent Years

FOR ALL PRACTICAL PURPOSES, THE *TITANIC* HAD FALLEN OFF THE EDGE OF THE EARTH.

Her general location was known—400 miles south of Newfoundland and 1,000 miles east of Boston—but the ship's resting place under a towering column of freezing water was as inaccessible as the moons of Jupiter.

However, as soon as the North Atlantic closed over her stern plates, men were scheming how to find and salvage her. Within weeks, representatives of the Astors, Wideners, and Guggenheims, the wealthiest families on board, met in New York to discuss a salvage contract with the marine engineers of Merritt and Chapman. The engineers studied the proposal, considered the heart-swelling sum of money behind it, and reluctantly said no. The wreck was too far from land. The weather was too unpredictable. The water was too deep. Even if they could find the *Titanic* in all those miles of water, she was too heavy to be raised.

In 1912, access into the ocean was limited. Most dives were made by men in vulcanized suits covered with heavy canvas twill. Strapped into stout leather boots and bolted into copper helmets, they clutched their lifelines, prayed that their hand-cranked air pumps would work, and jumped over the side. They sank like stones.

At that time, United States Navy divers were restricted to working depths of 60 feet. Merritt and Chapman divers couldn't go much deeper. The only thing that could reach into the depths that held the *Titanic* was human imagination.

Dreamers were charmed by the challenge. They pulled out their charts of the North Atlantic, opened their copies of Bowditch, and bent over their drafting tables. Charles Smith, a Denver architect, drew up an intricate plan that called for a deep-diving submarine, a crew of 162 men, and a cargo hold full of electromagnets. The magnets would find the ship's hull. Lift winches on a fleet of barges would haul the wreck to the surface. However, the last page of Smith's proposal held an item as deadly to its success as a depth charge—a cost of $1.5 million.

THE TREASURE SHIP

As the decades passed, the ghost ship in the foothills of the Grand Banks became synonymous with treasure. While no entries in the ship's manifest supported this, nothing accelerates treasure fever

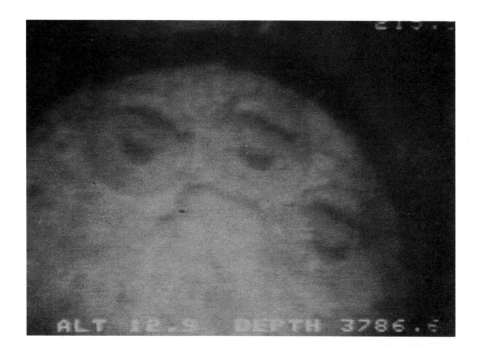

ALT 12.9   DEPTH 3786.5

catch up with the dream. As a new frontier, the deep ocean was as compelling as it was uncertain and unsettling. Its pioneers, a ragtag band of divers and submariners, confronted its enlivening interior with a combination of determination and dread.

By 1934, an American naturalist, Dr. William Beebe, and his colleague, Otis Barton, were gazing out a steamy porthole from inside a steel sphere 2,850 feet under the blue Atlantic near Bermuda. Thirty years later the loss of the nuclear submarine USS *Thresher* accelerated the need for men in submersibles to work at depths greater than 8,000 feet. By 1980, the technological options for exploring the deep ocean were sufficiently advanced to begin, with some prospect for success, a serious search for the *Titanic*.

more quickly than a lost luxury liner with a blue-ribbon passenger list. Supposition replaced reality. Somewhere, inside the hull or on the seafloor, so the story went, was a fabulous hoard of gold bullion, silver bars, diamonds, and pearls.

As the size of the alleged treasure expanded, so did the dementia of the dreamers. Anything that was buoyant and might lift a submerged object was worked into a salvage scheme and published in technical journals and Sunday supplements. The list included compressed air, canvas bags containing petroleum jelly, polyurethane foam, ice, ping-pong balls, and hydrogen gas from the electrolysis of seawater.

Salvaging the *Titanic* became a challenge for everyone, amateur and professional. And why not? No one could be proven wrong. All the dreamers were shielded by the same brutal physics that hindered Merritt and Chapman.

THE TECHNOLOGICAL IMPERATIVE

It was the great engine of the century, the technological imperative, that allowed the dreamers to

DISCOVERY

In the summer of 1980, "Cadillac Jack" Grimm sailed out from Fort Lauderdale on his first expedition. He failed to find anything, but by 1983, he and his teams had logged three summers' experience with winds, waves, currents, seafloor morphology, and deep-towed vehicles, a great benefit to any who followed his route into the North Atlantic.

In 1985, a French-American expedition, supported by millions of dollars and detailed topographic charts from the U.S. Navy, spent most of July and August looking for the *Titanic*. They were reasonably certain their target lay within a 100-square-mile area. The French, under the direction

of Jean Louis Michel in the ship *Le Suroit*, searched 80 percent of the designated seafloor without success. The American team, in the Woods Hole research vessel *Knorr* and under the direction of Bob Ballard, used a new deep-sea photo-imaging system to look for the scattered debris trail. On September 1, at 1:20 A.M., a television screen in the *Knorr*'s control van lit up with a blurred picture of one of the *Titanic*'s boilers. The Mount Everest of shipwrecks, which like Prohibition and the Depression had helped define the century, was about to begin a new phase of its existence.

A rat-tail fish swims past a collection of wine bottles and a chamber pot in the debris field. When the Titanic *struck the ocean floor, it sent up a plume of sediment that eventually settled in vessels such as these. Geological studies indicate that in this part of the ocean, sedimentation rates are very low.*

FACING *The blurred video image of a boiler face that confirmed the discovery of the* Titanic. *Made by the French-American team on September 1, 1985, the image revealed that as the* Titanic *broke up, this boiler was ejected from the bottom of the ship. It sank and landed faceup in the debris field.*

Mir 1 *is launched into the North Atlantic on one of the rare good-weather days. Weighing 18 tons, the sub holds a crew of three and can dive to a depth of 18,000 feet. Slung under its teardrop shape is a high-capacity battery system that allows it to remain underwater twice as long as other submersibles.*

FACING *David Bushnell's* Turtle

The Time Machines

FOR ALMOST 300 YEARS, MARINE ENGINEERS HAVE BEEN TRYING TO PERFECT SMALL, MAN-CARRYING SUBMARINES.

They were inspired by the fact that the human body, with its soft skin and delicate lungs, is not designed to exist outside the narrow envelope of air surrounding the earth. As we descend deeper into the sea, we are exposed to a murderous gallery of hazards, including hypoxia, gas embolism, decompression sickness, and hypothermia.

In 1718, in the new town of St. Petersburg, the Russian inventor Yefim Nikonov proposed the construction of a submerged and secret vessel. Two years later he launched a small, wooden, cigar-shaped seacraft into the muddy waters of the river Neva. One of the spectators was the Czar Peter the Great, a man obsessed with the vision of Russia as a world sea power. The first Russian submarine was designed "to destroy ships by projectiles." It slid through the water 50 years before David Bushnell's *Turtle* was built in America.

Before the 1917 revolution, the United States and Russia were occasional blue-water allies. American naval hero John Paul Jones, as a volunteer rear admiral in the Imperial Russian Navy, commanded a victorious squadron of frigates in the Black Sea. At the turn of the century, Joseph Holland and Simon Lake, the premier American submarine

designers, were highly influential in Russian submarine development. In 1904, Lake refitted his American-built sub, the *Protector*, and shipped it across the Atlantic to the Russian Navy.

However, since the 1950s, a radioactive curtain has been drawn in the sea between the two nations. For nearly half a century, fleets of nuclear-powered submarines crammed with nuclear-tipped warheads have engaged in a silent, electronic war. One of the small victories against this ongoing conflict has been won by a pair of Russian deep-diving research submersibles. Painted orange and white, they are 25 feet long, two feet shorter than Simon Lake's *Protector*.

THE NEW SUBS ARE BUILT

In 1985, after ten years of experience diving with two small Canadian-built seacraft, the Soviet Academy of Sciences in Moscow decided to design and build two new research submersibles. They are the best of the breed. Built at a cost of $25 million, each sub can carry a three-person crew to 18,000 feet, a depth that allows access to 95 percent of the oceans. The Russians call them *Mir 1* and *Mir 2*. In Russian, "mir" means peace.

Mir 1 *back in its tie-down cradle after a successful dive. Kneeling on top of the sub, Nikolai Petko completes a check of the emergency beacon. In the background, the white arm of the launch-and-recovery crane is poised to recover* **Mir 2.**

FACING *Aboard the* **Keldysh,** *the twin submersibles,* **Mir 1** *and* **Mir 2,** *with their orange topsides, rest alongside the railing aft of the smokestack. The weather-protection hangars are in the raised position.*

Each *Mir* weighs 18 tons. Their teardrop-shaped hulls are built around four spheres of high-yield nickel steel. The largest sphere, seven feet across, holds the crew of three and the gauges, switches, and electronics that control the life-support, communication, and hydraulic power systems. The other spheres carry seawater for ballast and trim. Power comes from a bank of ferronickel batteries slung under the hull. The *Mir*s can dive together, hover at any depth, and slip through the sea at a speed of five knots.

The two *Mir*s are operated by the P. P. Shirshov Institute of Oceanology in Moscow. Located 15 minutes from the golden spires of the Kremlin, the Institute is the most important center for ocean studies in Russia. Its staff of 2,000 scientists and tech-

nicians, marine biologists, geologists, physicists, chemists, and hydrographers work in laboratories and ships based in St. Petersburg, Moscow, Kaliningrad, and the Black Sea. The *Mir*s are housed on board the flagship of the fleet, the *Akademik Keldysh*, a floating Russian city block, its tiered superstructure holding 18 laboratories, 65 staterooms, and 130 people.

The twelve-man team that dives and maintains the *Mir*s is led by Dr. Anatoly Sagalevitch, 51, a marine engineer from Moscow. Head of the laboratory of manned submersibles at the Shirshov, he has devoted more than ten years of his life to building the world's best research subs and the technical team to support them.

In 1988, the Soviet Academy invited Western scientists to share the benefits of this new technology. The breeze that blew open the curtain was science. Long before the Berlin Wall was pulled down, the Russians were offering an opportunity to share the discoveries made during a series of dives. The long and dangerous descents would be made into a deep trough in the eastern section of the North Atlantic.

THE FIRST EXPEDITIONS

In June of 1989, under Sagalevitch's direction, ten dives were made into King's Trough, a submarine canyon north of the Azores. Running east to west, the sides of the highly irregular canyon are cut up by draws, gullies, and ravines. With a surgeon's patience and a pair of mechanical ma-

Emory Kristof (right) and Anatoly Sagalevitch inside Mir 1 *with the author at 16,400 feet. This dive, into King's Trough in the eastern North Atlantic, took place two years before the* Titanic *expedition.*

nipulators, the Russian pilots and diving geologists recovered dozens of dark, well-knit rocks deposited, cemented, and solidified some 25 million years ago. On one dive, a simulated extreme-depth rescue mission, the subs came together at a depth of three miles. Overhead were walls higher than the Grand Canyon. Above that was another mile and a half of water. The link-up occurred where pressure hulls begin to shudder, a place five times deeper than two subs had ever met before. Inside the mirror-image machines, looking out at each other through ice-cold portholes, were six men from three nations.

The scientific dives, so deep into the abyss of a perverse and unpredictable ocean, fathered a fragile union between two teams and their technologies: the Russians with their globe-circling ship and its two submersibles, and the North Americans with their gleaming complement of deep-sea cameras. The cameras were the inspired concept of Emory Kristof, a *National Geographic* photographer from Washington, D.C. A year later, Sagalevitch and Kristof joined forces in two more major expedi-

tions, using their synergistic machines to film swarms of rat-tail fish and other bizarre animals 18,000 feet under the Indian Ocean, and later in the year, to discover a series of hot water vents at the bottom of the world's deepest lake in Siberia. The spirit of John Paul Jones was alive and well inside the heart of the ocean.

To some, the ongoing expeditions, with 130 former Cold War adversaries working shoulder to shoulder on the decks of a seagoing village, represented a hopeful glimpse of the future. A group of human beings had discovered that shared risk and laughter have no language barrier. They had also learned that the best way to defeat your enemy is to turn him into your friend.

A view from inside Mir 2, looking up the deck of the Keldysh. The arms holding the HMI lights have been folded inward. In the background is the operator's cab of the launch-and-recovery crane.

From left to right, IMAX production crew members Paul Mockler, Per-Inge Schei, and Stephen Low line up a night shot in front of Mir 1. In the foreground is the National Geographic still camera, mounted on an articulating arm.

FACING **Mir 1,** *with its whisker booms extended and all lights turned on, cruises slowly over the seafloor.*

50

CHAPTER SIX

Capturing the Sun

IN 1967, FOUR CANADIAN FILMMAKERS DECIDED TO CREATE A SCREEN IMAGE SO LARGE THAT THE AUDIENCE WOULD FEEL ITSELF A PART OF THE FILM.

Unsurpassed in color and clarity, the images would be enhanced by a six-channel concert sound system. To stretch the mind and imagination of the audience into this exploded frame, the edges of the screen would lie beyond the maximum peripheral vision of the human eye. In a deft twist of tongue, the Canadians called their concept IMAX.

To ensure audience immersion into the film, they used the largest film frame in motion-picture history, ten times the size of a conventional 35-mm movie frame, and projected it onto a giant screen seven stories high. To accommodate this visual expanse they built theaters in which the audience would sit in steeply pitched rows so that everyone, children included, would have a full and perfect view of the picture.

The key to the stunning sharpness and stability of the IMAX image was the most powerful movie projector ever built. It consumed enough electricity—15,000 watts—to light a five-story building. The light blasting through its wide-angle lens was generated by a solar simulator xenon lamp. But the unique performance of the new

projector was brought about by a rolling loop, which advanced the film horizontally in a smooth, wavelike motion.

Two decades later, the Canadian dream had turned into a small global industry. In 15 countries, including the United States, Germany, France, and Japan, more than 80 IMAX theaters were built. Every year, at least 31 million people lined up outside these theaters to see one of the 80-plus IMAX films. Around the world dozens of producers, directors, cameramen, and technicians were working on new natural history or science-adventure projects. The privately held company, with its head office in a converted two-story Edwardian townhouse in Toronto and a new, multi-million-dollar technology facility nearby, had subsidiary offices in the United States, Europe, and Japan.

By 1989, the big black IMAX cameras had been everywhere: north of the Arctic Circle, under the canopy of the Amazon rain forest, strapped to the tail of a Lockheed L-1011, and peering through the window of the space shuttle as it orbited the earth. The one place its lenses

had never captured was the extreme edge of the abyss.

THE COMMITMENT

Then came the summer of 1990. It was a warm June day in Toronto, and down at the lake, the air was clear and brilliant with sunshine. Late in the morning, two Russians and three Canadians walked across a white steel bridge into the Ontario Place IMAX theater. One of the Russians and his Canadian friend had been inside a *Mir* submersible when it made the three-mile free fall into King's Trough. The other two Canadians had visions of new frontiers for the IMAX format. Alone in the darkened theater, the five men watched a film that propelled them down a mountainside at 60 miles an hour with an Olympic skier, into the air on satin point with a Kirov ballerina, and inside the hidden chambers of the human body.

The film, *To The Limit*, also drew their imaginations into the sea. At the end of the day they agreed to commit themselves to an IMAX film on the *Titanic*.

The financial risks, measured in millions, would be as vertiginous as the walls of King's Trough. A complementary science program would have to be organized. The two *Mir* submersibles would have to be reconfigured toward new levels of performance. But of all the dozens of technical obstacles, the most challenging was that a completely new deep-sea lighting system would have to be built.

Looking out of Mir 2 *through its central viewport as the sub is gently lowered into the water. The men in the towboat will free the line from under the HMI lights before they pull the sub clear of the ship.*

FACING *Each sub was equipped with four HMI lights, which illuminated the* Titanic *with the equivalent of about 150,000 watts of incandescent light (1,500 domestic 100-watt light bulbs). High in the blue and green end of the spectrum, the lights were ten times more powerful than any previously used on the* Titanic.

SUNLIGHT IN THE SEA

The quantity of sunlight pouring down on the sea depends on a number of factors, including cloud cover, time of day, and distance from the equator. As sunlight penetrates the wave tops, it is altered by reflection, refraction, and the billions of invisible particles and organic material suspended within the water that absorb and diffuse the light on its downward path. At 500 feet, sunlight fades to a purple twilight. The depths beyond 3,000 feet are forever black.

The secret pit of the ocean holds a universe of entangled infinities: perpetual cold, enduring pressure, a darkness measured in hundreds of millions of years. Here, when a submarine light is switched on, its beam is quickly swallowed. The longest wavelengths—red, orange, and yellow—disappear first. Twenty feet out from the point of incandescent fire, everything appears green, and beyond that, merges swiftly into obsidian black.

To project the *Titanic* life-size on a 70-foot screen meant lighting an enormous fluorescent bonfire two-and-a-half miles under the ocean. To solve this problem, the technical team, led by Chris Nicholson of Deep-Sea Systems and Mark Olsson of Deep Sea Power and Light, borrowed an idea from Hollywood. Three years earlier, the Osram Corporation of Germany had won an Oscar for the high-intensity HMI lights it had built for the feature film industry. Like the ordinary mercury-vapor streetlight, the Osram bulb contained two electrodes driving a hot arc of electricity through a gas-filled envelope. However, 23 years ago, Osram discovered that if the arc shot through a poisonous brew of mercury, thalium, and iodide, it produced a multispectral brilliance similar to sunlight. Over the years, a forest of Osram "sun guns" appeared in the back lots of Columbia and Paramount. However, no one had ever taken this technology and wired it into a deep-diving submarine.

PREPARING FOR THE EXPEDITION

Hundreds of technical problems had to be re-

solved in under five months. In Los Angeles, San Francisco, and Woods Hole, a swarm of technicians began assembling several hundred parts, including glass pressure housings, lamp bases, electrical-ballast circuit boards, aluminum flood reflectors, and solid-state switching panels. The Osram bulbs were rebuilt to make them smaller and then slipped inside test-tube-shaped glass enclosures. The igniter coils and flicker-free ballast were packed inside high-strength glass ceramic housings. In the final assembly, four HMI lights would be mounted on two whisker booms that would swing out from the bow of each sub like antennae on a communications satellite. Everything—igniters, lights, ballast, and booms—would be controlled

by the crew inside the submersible.

In some ways, it is easier to get humans into and out of a submersible than it is high-voltage electricity. Confronted with a mixture of water and steel, electrons rage and wander. To pass the power cables from the batteries and lights through two inches of steel meant using a custom-fabricated, through-the-hull penetrator with dual O-rings. But if the penetrator failed and current built up, a bolt of lightning might be unleashed.

One possibility was that the interior of the sub would become the negative terminal of a new electrical grid, the positive pole the exterior bank of 100-kilowatt batteries. The three men inside would feel their skin prickle and their hair stand on end. They

Mir 1 *taking still pictures and videotaping the embedded bow of the* Titanic *for the CBS television special* "Titanic: *Treasure of the Deep." Producer/director Al Giddings recorded some 30 hours of underwater footage for the historic program.*

FACING *As they prepare for a dive, filmmaker Stephen Low (left) and sub pilot Genya Chernyaev talk strategy inside Mir 2. In front of the center port is the 100-pound IMAX camera on its aluminum frame. A master at his trade, Chernyaev had to steer the 18-ton sub while looking through a side viewport.*

would hear a fizzing sound, then a crackling like a burning fuse. An instant later, the sphere would fill with a blue-white light and a jarring crash, as if the sub had been thrown onto a sidewalk. Another possibility was that the penetrator would melt through, the sea would pour in, and the occupants would perish within seconds. On the other hand, if the lights worked, they would splash brilliant beams of simu-

The Woods Hole Oceanographic video camera inside its high-pressure housing. Mounted on the starboard side of Mir 1, *the camera was a three-chip BetaCam specially modified by Sony for the expedition.*

FACING *The bow of* Mir 1, *with pilot Genya Chernyaev looking out through the center viewport. Above him are ballast spheres 2 and 3. In the foreground, on the mechanical arm, is the* National Geographic *35-mm still camera with its video "eyes" and strobe light.*

lated sunlight—equivalent to more than 500 automobile headlights—across the deck of the *Titanic*.

Mounting the 100-pound IMAX camera and its 230 pounds of film and accessories inside the sub posed another challenge. For optical reasons, the camera lens had to be as close as possible to the central viewport, but, to prevent damage, it could not touch it. For safety reasons, the mount had to allow for quick removal of the camera. Based on drawings and measurements, Imax engineers Gordon Harris and Bill Reeve developed a slim aluminum frame rigid enough to secure the camera during impacts up to six Gs. To allow the sub pilot to steer when his view was blocked by the outside equipment, Harris would install a tiny video camera and two monitors.

Ten months after the Ontario Place meeting, the primary elements of a major expedition were in place. A contract had been signed with the Russians. Financing had been arranged by André Picard and Michael McGrath at Imax. Steve Blasco of the Geological Survey of Canada was brought in as chief scientist. And producer/director Stephen Low was working on the outline of his giant-screen film, *Titanica*.

Somewhere in the turbulence of last-minute preparations, the team decided to convert the second *Mir* into an electronic sweatshop. To make a series of 35-mm stills for *National Geographic*, photographer Emory Kristof would install his camera, its aluminum housing, and a pair of three-dimensional video "eyes." To film the underwater scenes for his CBS television special, filmmaker Al Giddings would add an advanced three-chip Sony BetaCam inside a cylindrical high-pressure housing. The front of the sub would look like a heavy-metal ad for media America. The interior, jammed with digital readouts and video monitors, would look like an intensive care unit. The team hoped that the array of new lights and cameras on both subs would capture a slice of human history and set the technical standards for the next century. By spring, 1991, in cities across North America and the Soviet Union, a small group of men was preparing to sail to an unmarked place in the North Atlantic and dive with a pair of time machines.

The **Keldysh** *tied up at Pier 14 during a port call at St. Johns, Newfoundland.*

FACING ***Hundreds of vent shrimp with bright infrared sensors swarm over a smoking chimney at 10,000 feet on the Mid-Atlantic Ridge.***

CHAPTER SEVEN

New Faces on the Foredeck

ON THE EVENING OF MAY 15, 1991,
THE SOVIET RESEARCH SHIP *AKADEMIK KELDYSH* LEFT GERMANY
TO BEGIN THE MOST
EXPENSIVE AND COMPLEX
DEEP-DIVING EXPEDITION
EVER CONDUCTED.

More than 100 boxes and crates containing cameras, film, and spare parts were stowed below her decks. Her two-month charter had cost $1.5 million. The IMAX film added another $5 million. Factoring in the cost of the CBS television special, the *National Geographic* team, and the contingency expenses necessary for a two-month expedition, the total cost exceeded $7 million.

THE FIRST STOP

After steaming through the English Channel, the *Keldysh* turned southwest and headed toward a point in the Atlantic midway between the cities of Miami in the U.S. and Dakar in Senegal. Five days later, she stopped to confirm her position. Ten thousand feet below her keel lay the central rift valley of the Mid-Atlantic Ridge. Within the steeply pitched walls of the valley, sprawling across five square miles, was the underwater equivalent of Yellowstone Park.

In the perpetual darkness of the abyss was a smoking field of hot springs. The hottest of the springs, rumbling up through steeple-shaped chimneys, blew out a sulfurous column of smoke at 365° C, a temperature that melts lead. As they cooled and settled, the smoke plumes laid down thick deposits of minerals, including copper and zinc. During the thousands of years that this dragon's breath had been roaring up from the center of the earth, it had built an irregular mound the size of the Houston Astrodome.

The following day, the two *Mir*s were lifted over the starboard side of the *Keldysh*. After pausing on the surface, they dropped for two hours, and then steered toward one of the vents. The first time the IMAX camera was switched on and focused at this depth, it captured a scene as puzzling as the improbable pupfish that live on the sunbaked floor of Death Valley: thick clouds of shrimp, millions of them, gray, eyeless, and two inches long. They were twitching, pulsing, banging into each other, rejoicing in the heat. To allow them to cling to their permanent sauna, evolution has gifted them with an infrared sensor, a small reflective patch they wear on their backs.

The next stop for the *Keldysh* was St. George's, Bermuda, where the rest of the crew joined the ship. The new HMI

Russian engineer Nickolai Petko has removed a side panel from **Mir 2** *to check the sub's hydraulic system.*

RIGHT **Mir 1** *makes a night dive to 50 feet in Bermuda to check out the new lighting system. Kneeling in the sand, Stephen Low films the dive with the IMAX camera in its underwater housing.*

lighting system was mounted on both subs and tested in 50, 100, and 8,000 feet of water. During the deeper dives off the north slope of the Bermuda seamount, the Russian scientists discovered igneous rocks that yielded new information about this part of the Atlantic.

On the second day out of Bermuda, as the ship headed north, the sky turned black. Winds gusted to 50 knots. Waves broke green over the bow, their hoary crests slamming into the bridge windows 50 feet above sea level. Thirty-eight hours later, the *Keldysh* entered the funereal waters that held the *Titanic*.

ON LOCATION

41° 46'N, 50° 14'W. According to Fourth Officer Boxhall, these coordinates were the last known position of the *Titanic*. Over the years they became the best-known latitude and longitude in maritime history. But, as the four *Titanic* search expeditions were to discover, the coordi-

nates were wrong. The disabled *Titanic* had plunged to the bottom 12 miles to the southeast.

This was where the *Keldysh* now coasted, confirming her location by interpreting signals streaming down from a global positioning satellite. The next morning she dropped her own cluster of "satellites," four tubular transponders that landed upright on the ocean floor to form an electronic fence around the wreckage.

Lashed into its steel cradle on board the *Keldysh*, a *Mir* sub looks draconic, a mechanical beast with three eyes and two folded arms. The eyes are a trio of viewports in the bow, each the size of a saucer. The retractable arms, encircled by cables and hydraulic lines, are attached to both sides of the hull. Behind them, running aft to the stern propeller, is a network of control, communication, and propulsion systems.

The predive checklist for the *Mir* was as time-consuming as the one for the Mercury spacecraft. Before each dive, a dozen Russians inspected

every inch of pipe and plating, looking for weaknesses in the beast's technical armor. The flaws they couldn't see worried them the most: microscopic corrosion that might invade and weaken the pressure hull, a faulty wire, hidden behind a panel, that might overheat. Inside the manned sphere were 2,000 electrical connections and a mile of wire. Even a small fire meant smoke and heat that had nowhere to go except inside the crew's lungs.

Mir 2 in mid-recovery after a dive. Mir 1 is already in its cradle on board the Keldysh. Both weather-protection hangars are in the raised position.

Splashdown! **Mir 2** *hits the water in a rough-weather launch. The "Russian cowboys" race in to release the sub from its lift-line before the arrival of the next wave.*

During a recovery, Leonid Volchek locks the lift-line and prepares to leap back into the oncoming Zodiac.

PROFILE OF A DIVE

The *Mir*s are lifted into the sea by a 20-ton crane located between the subs on the deck of the *Keldysh*. Each launch takes about eight minutes. The tie-down cables are removed, the crane's lift-line is tightened, and the 18-ton sub is hoisted over the rail. Because the *Keldysh* is almost always rolling in the swells, the sub begins to sway. Using wooden tackles and lines as tight as marlin spikes, the ten-man launch crew tries to steady it. Slowly the crane extends its arm and releases its charge to the heaving sea. When the *Mir* enters the ocean, the water around it boils. Within seconds, a young Russian in bare feet and a wet suit leaps from a darting Zodiac onto the back of the sub. With the sea foaming around his knees, he reaches down and unlocks the lift-line. In big waves, if his timing is off, the sub and the ship will collide.

To conserve the limited power supply, the *Mir* pilot adds water to the ballast spheres and rides downward on gravity's pull. In the manned sphere, under

lights that have been dimmed, the pilot and co-pilot check their sustaining systems: oxygen flow, carbon dioxide level, battery reserves, hydraulic pressures, and downward drift relative to the transponders. On the surface, inside the main-deck command room of the *Keldysh*, four men bend over charts and computers to reconfirm the sub's position and talk to the pilot. By the time the first *Mir* is at 3,000 feet, the second is in the water, following its twin's acoustic trail.

It takes about three hours to make the two-and-a-half-mile trip to the bottom. At the end of the descent, about 500 feet above the seafloor, the pilot pumps water out of the ballast sphere. As the rate of descent slows, the manned sphere becomes quiet, and three pairs of eyes scan the data coming from the forward-looking sonar and digital depth sounder. Two hundred feet from touchdown, the co-pilot switches on the low-intensity survey lights. Seen from the viewports, the seafloor—tawny, featureless, and flat—seems to be rising to meet the sub. The pilot turns on the vertical thrusters. Imperceptibly, like a

RIGHT *Bronze telemotor steering control. The wooden steering wheel, last used by helmsman Robert Hitchans as he swerved the ship "hard-a-starboard," has gone.*

FACING *The 7³/₄-ton port bow anchor still secure in its hawsepipe. There is much less corrosion around this anchor than the one on the starboard side.*

giant tortoise easing into the mud, the *Mir* engages the seafloor of the North Atlantic.

After a quick conversation with the second sub, the pilot lifts the *Mir* off the bottom and begins steering a course to confirm the "ground-truth" of his position. Working from a mental map of the wreck site and looking for landmarks, he moves the *Mir* forward at a speed no faster than a man can walk. As soon as he sees something he recognizes, he will reset his course for the rendezvous point. Meanwhile, far above, the second sub glides down through the currents.

THE FIRST DIVE

The first dive in *Mir 1* was made on June 30 by Anatoly Sagalevitch, Emory Kristof, and Al Giddings. Shortly after noon they were at maximum depth, creeping forward on a heading of 300 degrees. Their forward-looking sonar had stopped working. About an hour later they almost ran into the intact forward section of the *Titanic*—a black escarpment of rusting steel 470 feet long from the bow to the break. At four o'clock, after surveying

the bow and forecastle deck, they parked on the bridge. The wooden walls and windows of the wheelhouse were gone. The roof was open to the full weight of the ocean. Directly in front of the sub, under the buttery glare of the HMI lights, was the steering telemotor, the bronze pedestal that once held the ship's wheel.

In the darkness 40 feet below them, *Mir 2* was taking closeup pictures of the 7³/₄-ton port anchor suspended in its hawsepipe. Inside the sub, pilot Genya Chernyaev, cameraman Ralph White, and technician Bill Reeve were shooting the first 3,000 feet of high-definition IMAX film. White was surprised at the amount of corrosion that had formed since his last dives to the *Titanic* four years earlier. Hanging from the hull plates like a garden of loose vines were orange-red rusticles, formed by corrosion and gravity and shaped by currents.

The first dive ended prematurely. *Mir 1*'s main propulsion unit jammed. *Mir 2* snapped its starboard HMI light bar. At one-thirty the next morning, both submersibles had risen like smoke to the high rim of the ocean and been lifted back on board the *Keldysh*.

SEVENTEEN DIVES IN SEVENTEEN DAYS

Between June 30 and July 16, seventeen dives were made to the scattered ruins of the *Titanic*. Eleven dives concentrated on the intact forward section; six concentrated on the stern. A total of 20 men spent 139 hours on the bottom. Stephen Low, Ralph White, and Paul Mockler shot 40,000 feet of IMAX film. Emory Kristof and Al Giddings took 600 stills and 50 hours of 3-D and broadcast-quality video. Lev Moskalev, Yuri Bogdanov, and Steve Blasco collected a year's worth of biological samples, sediment cores, and scientific impressions.

Behind the actuarial summaries are some simple truths. A big ship, especially one the size of the *Titanic*, is an iron trap for submersibles. Loose wires, torn metal, and sawtooth openings hidden in darkness and unpredictable currents can be deadly. Every sub pilot knows how two young men were killed when the *Johnson-Sealink* was pinned to the bottom near Key West. Several of the dives to the *Titanic* provided moments of spiked adrenaline. On one dive, a sudden current swept *Mir 1* along the starboard side of the bow section and under the fractured lower decks where the ship had broken in two. On another descent, *Mir 2* jammed its skids behind a low railing

on the shelter deck: it took eight minutes for the pilot to work the sub free. On perhaps the most dramatic dive of the series, *Mir 1* and *Mir 2* dove under the stern of the *Titanic*, easing themselves down an incline to film the bronze blades of the starboard propeller. Hanging over their heads was 25 feet of time-weakened steel.

A second truth is that the six Russian pilots and co-pilots—Anatoly Sagalevitch, Genya Chernyaev, Victor Nischeta, Andrei Andreev, Nikolai Shushkov, and Anatoly Blagodaryov—are as skilled in their craft as surgeons. Including the hours required for descents and ascents, the two *Mir*s were underwa-

The two **Mir** *subs dive under the overhanging stern to film the starboard wing propeller. Inside* **Mir 2**, *the IMAX camera is running (see photograph on page 2). The straight skid tracks in the sediment show how close* **Mir 1** *came to the propeller.*

FACING **Mir 1** *gliding at a speed of about 1 knot over the bow toward the bridge. The port and starboard anchor windlass drums are in the foreground. The chain cables feeding through these two windlasses weigh 96 tons and have a length of 330 fathoms (1,980 feet).*

ter for two weeks. Although much of this time was spent prowling a neighborhood festooned with wire and cable, with one sub half-blinded by an IMAX camera blocking the main viewport, there were no operational emergencies.

Every night, the Russian surface crew set aside the need for sleep and climbed in and out of the subs, recharging batteries, replenishing oxygen, keeping the *Mir*s working like a pair of Swiss watches. Canadian and American technicians toiled beside them, paying the same obsessive attention to their deep-sea cameras and lights. The preoccupation paid off. During the dives, there were no time-consuming technical problems.

In its own sullen way, the North Atlantic was intermittently cooperative. Fog paid an occasional visit. On some days the sun broke through the clouds and helped guide the subs into the water. During the 17 days the *Keldysh* was on station over the *Titanic*, four storms rich with lightning and thunder, rain and wind, swept through the area. The clouds that towered into night and the yellow stabs of lightning were a blessing to the pilots and crew, who tumbled into bed, confident that diving operations would be postponed for a few hours.

Urged by a constellation of motives that included science, filmmaking, storytelling, engineering, and just plain curiosity, eight Russians and 12 North Americans visited the *Titanic*. Each one carried memories of the experience as if they were diamonds in their pockets.

On the port side, just forward of the second funnel, the boat deck has fallen in on the promenade deck. The shape of the depression suggests that it might have been made by the funnel falling forward as the ship sank.

FACING *Night launch of* Mir 1. *On the left is the towboat, with its line attached to the bow of the sub. The launch of* Mir 2 *will follow within the hour.*

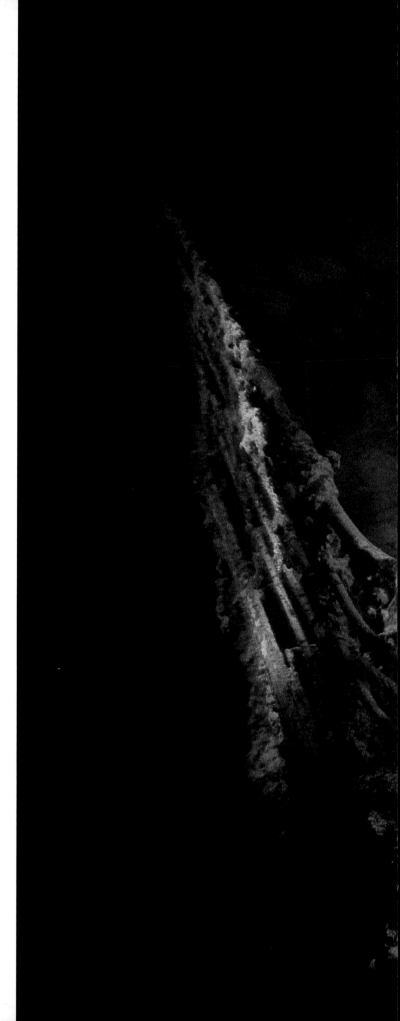

Looking down on the point of the bow. Just beyond the railing, in a well in the forecastle deck, is the ship's 15¹/₂-ton center anchor.

PAGES **72-73** *A pair of mooring bollards on the forecastle deck. The starboard railing, damaged during the tumultuous descent, is in the background.*

PAGES **74-75** *Steam-driven cargo winch on the forecastle deck between the number one and number two hatches. The winch was used to load cargo into the hold.*

*Open windows of the officers' quarters
facing out onto the starboard boat deck. To
the left is a steam-driven winch used to raise
the lifeboats during tests.*

Also on the starboard boat deck, but farther aft, is the wide, vertical cleft that was the forward expansion joint.

*Collection of wine bottles with corks still in place. In
the foreground, a purple gorgonian soft coral
reaches up into the currents for nutrients.*

*Assorted floor tiles, pots, and pieces of wood
in the debris field.*

*A suitcase with leather handles lies
upside down in the debris field.*

*A filigreed piece of a gold-plated candelabrum is picked up, photo-
graphed, and replaced by the mechanical arm of Mir 2.*

Lower part of the starboard main reciprocating engine. A white Galathea crab, about the size of a human hand, is standing on the horizontal pipe.

*Looking across the boat deck on the port side of
the bow section. The small object on the left is a
high-pressure water control valve.*

One after the other, the Mirs move in for a closeup view of the mysterious hole on the starboard side of the bow, near E deck.

The convex shape of the hull running along the bottom of the photograph suggests to some experts that the hole may have been produced by the explosive force of air trapped inside the sinking ship. The opening of the hole is about 15 feet by 20 feet and includes part of the frame of a loading port. Because they are "inside" the ship and protected from currents, the orange-red rusticles are the biggest yet seen. Beyond them are the outlines of several third-class decks.

The head of the high-pressure cylinder of the starboard main engine is four-and-a-half feet in diameter. The top of the cylinder is about five stories above the seafloor.

A large section of the outer hull lying on its side near the main engines. The six-foot horizontal division between the plates and a row of portholes is clearly visible. One of the largest pieces in the debris field, it came from the hull in the area between the second and third funnels.

PAGES 86-87 Another view of the forecastle deck, showing the descent-damaged railing and the fairleads used to guide heavy lines over the side to the mooring bollards. The wood from the deck has long since disappeared; only the caulking remains.

A large piece of steampipe lying in the sediments of the debris field. In the distance are the lights of Mir 1. The sediments under the Titanic and its debris field are very dense and more than a million years old. If normal ocean muds were present, heavy objects like this pipe would be buried.

FACING *A rat-tail fish hovers over a sediment-filled sink bowl, a wine bottle, and pieces of floor tile.*

CHAPTER EIGHT

Unlocking the Secrets

THIS WAS THE THIRD MANNED MISSION TO THE *TITANIC* SINCE IT WAS DISCOVERED IN 1985, BUT THE FIRST TO CONDUCT DETAILED BIOLOGICAL, GEOLOGICAL, AND METALLURGICAL STUDIES.

The 1986 Woods Hole expedition used the research submersible *Alvin* to make an 11-dive photo survey. A year later, the French government, financed by a group of American investors, made a series of dives in the submersible *Nautile* to salvage some 800 artifacts from the debris field.

The Imax-*Titanic* science program was an alliance between the Geological Survey of Canada and the Shirshov Institute in Moscow. During every dive, observations were made and pictures taken for their cinematic and scientific value. Three dives were devoted to scientists, who collected biological and geological samples. The articulating arms of the *Mir* submersibles were able to reach out and push 30-cm-long tubes into the sea floor to recover ten sediment core samples. In addition, Canada's senior research vessel, CSS *Hudson*, recovered a one-meter sediment core from the ancient, dense sediments of the valley floor near the wreck.

The four imaging technologies—35-mm stills, 3-D video, broadcast video, and IMAX—captured a dazzling spectrum of visual information. The two hours of IMAX footage, with each frame containing ten times as much information as a 35-mm frame, will

keep the scientists busy for years to come.

VIEWS OF THE WRECKAGE

The summary scientific report, written by chief scientist Steve Blasco and biologist Lev Moskalev, confirms a mutual admiration for the subtle dynamics of this part of the Atlantic Ocean.

Many thousands of years ago, a massive submarine landslide of fluidized mud, sand, and gravel tumbled down the continental slope and invaded the valley where the *Titanic* eventually came to rest. During the slow, steady march of geologic time, other landslides occurred, building up layers of hard rubble. When the forward section of the *Titanic* crash-landed—more than 20,000 tons moving at ten knots—it only penetrated the rubble to a depth of 40 feet. As it did so, it created a "bow wave" of seabed material some 30 feet high.

The *Titanic* wreckage is being swept by irregular bottom currents of a quarter to a half knot, with occasional gusts up to one knot. Coming from all directions, these currents scoop up the top layers of sediment and press them into slipface dunes and ripples.

Crabs, corals, shrimps, ane-

arctic Canada and western Greenland.

The first impression of the scientists who saw the *Titanic* was that it was rusting at a fairly substantial rate. Rows of rusticles hanging from all parts of the ship, piles of broken rusticles on the seabed near the hull, and rivers of rust flowing from the wreck all create the impression of an old ship dissolving into an enormous orange mound.

A scanning electron microscope was used to analyze the corrosion on five pieces of recovered metal and sections of rusticles. The microstructure of the rusticles and rust flakes from the metal indicate that in addition to chemical oxidation, bacteria play a major role in their formation. Cold, pressure, and the rust itself may be slowing the oxidation process. For the moment, no one knows.

HOW THE SHIP BROKE UP

New evidence from the debris field is being used to reconstruct the major events in the breakup of the ship. Structural calculations indicate that the *Titanic* was strong enough to support itself when, during the final moments, the stern rose out of the water. For some reason, during its death, the great ship lost a huge, V-shaped section including the third and fourth funnels. The contents of this missing section lie as twisted and fragmented pieces across a large area of the debris field.

The ship apparently came apart at the last boiler line. Four of the five boilers in this line are accounted for, but the fifth is missing. Not surprisingly, a boiler flooding with cold water and bursting apart at the seams is common in sinking ships: it happened to the *Titanic*'s sister ship *Britannic*. The findings suggest that during the final plunge, the fifth boiler may have exploded and contributed to the wrenching

mones, and starfish are some of the 28 known species of animals that have taken up residence on the wreck. Riding the currents above them are four species of fish, including the ghost-white, armor-headed rat-tail.

Icebergs have always cast their shadows over the graveyard of the *Titanic*. As arctic glaciers grind their way toward the sea, the moving ice incorporates underlying sediments, rocks, and boulders into its structure. Icebergs calved from these glaciers carry this dark debris with them. And, as they drift south into warmer water, they randomly release their cargo into the depths. Scattered throughout the ruins of the ship are small pieces of

Biologist Lev Moskalev and geologist Steve Blasco (right) study pieces of metal recovered from the Titanic *site. On the left is part of a hull plate. The long piece is from a cast-iron deck beam. Five pieces of metal and some rusticles were the only items removed from the site during the expedition.*

FACING *Two views of the same cast-iron frame of a deck bench. The upper photograph was taken in 1986. The lower one, taken five years later, shows that the stream of rust has advanced to the bottom of the frame.*

apart of the hull. It appears that a combination of bending and tensile stresses fractured the ship on the surface, sending fragments of hull plates, beams, decks, stairwells, and contents of the V-section drifting down to the alluvial floor.

THE MYSTERIOUS BRITTLE METAL

During the tenth dive, a piece of metal the size of a soup plate was recovered by *Mir 2*. Its $^{7}/_{8}$-inch thickness, countersunk rivet holes, and lead oxide paint confirmed that it was a section of hull plate. Engineering impact tests carried out in a lab in Ottawa, Ontario, revealed that the metal, a product of Edwardian open-hearth furnaces, was brittle. Instead of bending under stress, it shattered. And it shattered easily. The reason for this unusual behavior was locked inside its molecular structure. The fragment of hull plate was coarse-grained and contained "stringers" of sulfide.

If a number of plates were plagued with such brittleness, it may help explain why the brush with the iceberg was so devastating. When struck, a single plate might shatter, but only as far as its edges. While water pouring in through one damaged plate could easily be handled by the ship's pumps, if the iceberg struck a series of plates, it might cause them to disintegrate, one after the other—in effect, opening up the side of the ship.

DEEP-OCEAN BENCHMARK

Lying at the ocean's average depth, the *Titanic* is an ideal benchmark. We know to the minute when this brand-new ocean liner went to the bottom. We know exactly how long she has been lying in her woeful valley. Each time we visit this drowned museum, we can observe and record the ongoing sea changes—the influence of the wreckage on its environment and the transformations taking place within the pieces of the submerged giant.

What we learn and capture on film about the *Titanic* can be compared to what we discover about other deep-ocean shipwrecks in the future. More than one tenth of all the ships that ever sailed have sunk in depths far below the reach of divers. Thousands of them are wooden ships, Phoenician and Greek, lost long before the Christian era. However, some of the most threatening to the future health of the oceans went down in the past few years. Among these are six nuclear submarines, four Russian and two American, whose plutonium fires are still burning.

For some time, conventional wisdom has held that the deep ocean, the outer edge of nowhere, was isolated and inert, an excellent burial ground for radioactive and toxic wastes. We now know that for all those places like the black, unremembered slopes of the *Titanic* valley, we will have to recalibrate our thinking.

Twice in its brief history, the *Titanic* has changed the way the world imagines the ocean. Her sudden death in 1912 inspired new safety regulations for the use of lifeboats and the surveillance of icebergs. Her discovery in 1985 and recent exploration by submersibles from three nations confirm that mankind has, after thousands of years of seafaring, built the technology to open the gates to the deep ocean. For better or worse, earth's final frontier has been breached.

Twisted hull plates and exposed inner frames of a badly damaged part of the stern section.

Russians, Canadians, and Americans turn out for a group portrait on the upper deck of the Keldysh.

Comrades of the Deep

WITH ITS RADIUM-COLORED LIGHTS, EXTREME-DEPTH TWIN SUBMERSIBLES, AND GIANT-SCREEN FILM,

THE IMAX-*TITANIC* EXPEDITION HAS CHANGED THE DYNAMICS OF DEEP-OCEAN EXPLORATION.

But the essence of the expedition was not the technology, the filming, or the science. It was 130 people fused into one community.

For the small group of men and women who spent part of a summer together in the shadows and fog of the North Atlantic, the Cold War never existed. In their curiosity about an old ship and the older ocean that embraces its wreckage, their thoughts had moved elsewhere. Inside their common experience was a brief moment when myth, fact, and maritime and political history fused together.

Most of all, as they flirted with the abyss, they cared about each other. For all of them, the expedition was more than a gathering of colleagues on a special assignment. It was a spiritual exercise. The dives they made together were dramatic, exhausting, challenging, and irresistible. For those who participated, or watched the events unfold, they represented one of the great moments in undersea exploration.

One of the expedition hard hats.

Titanic, *Belfast Lough, April 2, 1912.*

ABOUT THIS BOOK

TITANIC IN A NEW LIGHT is a companion book to the IMAX film *Titanica*, a Stephen Low Film produced by Low Films International Inc. for Imax Corporation. With the financial participation of the Export Development Corporation, Telefilm Canada, the Ontario Film Development Corporation, the Canadian Museum of Civilization, and Ontario Place Corporation. Completion bond provided by Motion Picture Guarantors, and performance bond provided by Zurich Indemnity.

The film *Titanica* is produced and directed by Stephen Low, with Pietro Serapiglia as co-producer and Dr. Joseph MacInnis and André Picard as executive producers.

The IMAX images were filmed by Stephen Low, Paul Mockler, and Ralph White supported by Gord Harris and Bill Reeve.

IMAX is a registered trademark of Imax Corporation, Toronto, Canada.

PHOTO CREDITS

Laura Aumanto/Geological Survey of Canada: pages 62-63, 63. Eva Hart family: page 34. Gail Harvey: page 91. From the IMAX Film *Titanica* © Imax Corporation/TMP (1991) I Limited Partnership: pages 4-5, 10, 21, 36, 38-39, 40, 41, 43, 47, 49, 51, 53, 64, 66, 69, 70-71, 72-73, 74-75, 78 (2), 79 (2), 80, 81, 82-83, 84, 85, 86-87, 88, 89, 92-93. Jeff MacInnis: page 19. Dr. Joseph MacInnis: pages 15, 23, 46, 52, 56, 60 (left). National Geographic Society/Emory Kristof: pages 12, 16, 20, 50, 54, 57, 60, 65, 67, 68, 76, 77, 90 (bottom). National Geographic Society/Dr. Joseph MacInnis: page 48. NOAA/Woods Hole/MIT: page 59. Ocean Images/Terry Thompson: page 61. Leonard G. Phillips: page 95. Charles Sachs: page 35. Ulster Folk & Transport Museum, Northern Ireland: pages 2-3, 6, 8, 22, 24-25, 26-27, 27 (2), 28, 29, 30, 31 (2), 32-33, 96. U.S. Naval Institute: page 45. Woods Hole Oceanographic Institution: pages 42, 90 (top). Yuri Volodin/Shirshov Institute of Oceanology: pages 37, 44, 55, 58, 94.

The author would like to thank Ken Anderson, Gayle Bonish, Michael Davies, Craig Dobbin, Bill Graves, Bill Hopper, Alex Low, and Teddy, Edna, and Wendy Tucker.